Styling by Faith

By

Tracey Moss

A CELEBRITY TV AND FILM HAIRSTYLIST'S GUIDE TO SECURING A WIN

Bryce Parker Publishing

First Edition: December 2019

Copyright © 2019 by Tracey Moss

All rights reserved.

No part of this book may be reproduced, scanned, or distributed in any printed or electronic form without permission.

ISBN - 781734012705

Printed in the United States of America

Dedication

To Bryce Smiley, my one and only son.

Your existence has ignited a fire of strength and courage that has caused an explosion in my life and has allowed me to leap further than I have ever imagined. I thought motherhood had passed for me, but God knew the ultimate goal for my life. I love you dearly, son..

To Edith Marie Johnson, my mother

You have unselfishly loved me from before birth. This dedication is for the many years you sacrificed your life so I can pursue my dreams. Your unconditional love and sound advice have fueled me into the woman, mother, hairstylist, author, dreamer, and God-loving woman I am today. There is no amount of love that can measure my love for you. Thank you, Mom.

Acknowledgments

First of all, I would like to thank my Heavenly Father, who has made all things possible, and I am grateful for Him in directing and shaping my life.

I would like to express my gratitude to the many people that contributed to the completion of this book.

My sincere thanks to Morshe Araujo and Gina Salmon of Killing It Write for seeing me through this project and by providing support, encouragement, and knowledge led by an undeniable level of professionalism. Thank you Lynn Williams for your valuable support in graphic design.

Special thanks to the photographer and videographer Tailah Breon for capturing the very essence of me on the cover of the book and on the trailer. Tailiah, you hold a special place in my heart. Standing in front of the eye of the lens, whether it's still prints or videos was not always easy for me. However, your attention to detail and God-given talent exemplifies your total greatness. I am thankful to you for being a part of my team.

I am forever grateful for Olivia Almagro for her loving support, patience, and her vital part in believing and assisting me in transforming my story into a book and introducing it to the world. You are a jewel, and I'm thankful for God's timing with the collaboration of you and me.

To my aunts, friends, family, and extended family, my deepest thank you for your continuous love, support, and prayers. The measure of faith God has given you all has been a great help to me. It has strengthened and enriched me. These individuals have encouraged me to seek newer and deeper territories in God, which came with a greater level of growth.

Mikki, you are my role model, and I thank you for inspiring me from birth.

To my aunt Ethel who is resting in peace, I cherish your love and timeless words of wisdom forever.

A special thanks to Terrence and Bryce Smiley, the dynamic duo who have allowed me the time and space to fulfill the assignment that God has called on my life in this season. Your patience not only for me working fourteen-hour days, but your love and support mean everything to me.

Table of Contents

Introduction	1
Chapter 1 Identify Your Gift	9
Chapter 2 A Position To Win	31
Chapter 3 Strategic Moves	45
Chapter 4 Trust The Process	53
Chapter 5 Take A Leap	65
Chapter 6 Get Connected	83
Chapter 7 Bet on Yourself	95
Chapter 8 The Power Within	101
Chapter 9 What's Next	109

Introduction

Do you have a dream? A little seed in your heart that's growing and dying to burst forth and flourish. Are you hindered by doubts, circumstances, and fear?

In this book, I outline the tools needed to recognize your dream and go after it. My hope is that readers will take away from this book, my sincere and genuine attempt to release the fire within you and to birth your vision.

For my go-getters, let's exhale and strategically map out a blueprint so that you can make purposeful power moves. You are going to get there. With or without me, I know it.

So, before you go bungee jumping headfirst first into your dreams, allow my journey to navigate and assist you toward accomplishing one or many of your desired goals, and to equip you with the knowledge required to tap into the supernatural ability that God has gifted each and every one of us. It will come effortlessly, that talent that comes easy to you and gets you superior results with the help of no one.

Styling by Faith is written and designed first for the millennial. The world is yours, and you're going to achieve and conquer the world. Nothing or no one can stand in your way. You will be your own boss, and you will have your own company in just a matter of time. Besides, why work for someone else when you have the skills and a network of people who can help you build your personal brand and start your company?

I wrote Styling by Faith for people like myself, and I'll explain why. There is no way I could've written this book, given the advice that you'll find between these pages, or helped assist anyone without incorporating the ideas and advice gathered for those who have traveled in a similar path as I have. For example, I went away to college, started a career and journey one way, my journey altered following a totally different leg of the path after that. Often, a drastic change mid-way leaves you feeling like you've wasted your money and time. Yes, you can incorporate your experience, but right now, you need to envision a clear direction.

Styling by Faith was also written in mind for the professional veteran who's been stuck in the same space for many years with a strong desire for change. This individual could follow their passion and dreams but doesn't have any idea of where to start or how to get there. There's a yearning desire that won't allow your spirit to rest because you know you're supposed to be somewhere else. The professional veteran has been doing the same thing for so long, and everything is so different. Technology, skills set, and the route to try to go after what you've been dreaming of is completely different from when you started.

Writing a book was not part of my vision. I never considered myself a writer, an English major, nor an author. I'm the chick with note pads everywhere, always losing one and having to purchase another. One of my best friends calls me "Ms. Technology." I'll have my computer, smartphones, and other devices all around me at any given time. I am a creative thinker; I see the world in art form—colors, shapes, and even numbers. Writing a book was the last thing I thought I could do, attempt, or possibly deliver, not to mention, complete.

I have held numerous positions. I am no different from you. I have a family. I'm a mother, daughter, aunt, friend, and a woman who trusts in God with every aspect of my life. I started out as a millennial with a CEO mindset, but with no Internet or technology to get there. I was a low-paid intern who assisted a lot of people, and I was determined to succeed. I was not aware of where I was going, and I had to reroute my plans. I was a hairstylist for more than twenty years. I knew nothing about technology. It's something I knew I had to learn, and I did. I am still working on achieving balance in my work and personal life, especially with a full career, a family, and a busy four-year-old son.

It is a true testament that I am publishing my book because I know to trust, listen, and believe that God's timing is the limit.

My career has taken me places I never imagined, dreamed, believed, invested, or planned. Television and film were a part of my dream and vision, but God's timing of allowing companies that produce film and television projects in Georgia to receive tax incentives couldn't have been better. This was good news for me. More projects filmed in Georgia meant more opportunities to style hair on production sets. I obtained enough workdays to qualify to become a member of the union. This was yet another miracle from God. After three years of putting in hours of work and following the proper steps, I became a member of the union on September 10, 2011. My TV and Film career finally came to fruition. I've also had the opportunity to work with well-known celebrities like Gabrielle Union, Regina Hall, and Monica, just to name a few.

This is my personal testimony, tangible evidence that all things are possible.

With the advent of the Internet, society has changed the measuring stick of success. Some of your goals came directly as a result of your inner-circle, community, work, environment, and now at the touch of a finger, you're exposed to a world of ideas.

Readers can expect to see and learn about what I call the "PIE" formula. Irrespective of what level you're on professionally and creatively, you're in the space of not knowing what to do and can't quite figure it out.

The P stands for Plan. I will provide tips and ideas on how to determine what you want to do in life and what you want to target and map out as you plan to achieve it.

The I is for invest. Investing is the most critical point of your application. The investing process deals with money, time, and people. Often, you can set a goal and take it on headfirst. However, you will learn the importance and the process of strategically invest. All doors and opportunities that come your way are not always good for your brand and your business.

Finally, E stands for Execute. Execution is where goals are met and where dreams are made. Execution is what's going to get your business off the ground. It's going to take you and your brand to the next level.

This book will give you details of my personal journey and get you to where you want to be, need to be, and deserve to be.

I also encourage readers to implement some of these strategies to their road map of success. Maybe like me, the path you originally embarked on in life didn't fuel the fire burning in your soul. Know that it is not too late. You have the courage to undo and redirect your path and walk in your purpose with confidence and a plan. No one has a desire to remain the same. We all have dreams and aspirations that we would like to achieve. Everyone is in a place or a position for promotion. It doesn't matter what level you're at in life.

I have specifically taken the time to formulate strategic steps to help you reach your desired goal. These steps are not based on the internet, bloggers, or the opinions of expert marketing gurus. These steps have been experimented and tested with blood, sweat, and tears. These steps are guaranteed to position you to succeed.

There's a story my mom loved to tell when I was a little girl. I was barely walking, but a circle had formed around me at the grocery store. I smiled and danced with people. "There is something about your personality," she said, "that causes people to gravitate toward you."

I am known as the peacemaker. A natural giver, and after a decade of being a hairstylist, I hope to earn a certification in counseling or goal setting. It's on its way, and I am calling it.

On a more serious note, I have the ability to birth gifts. It doesn't matter what field you're in or whether you have tapped into your path to success or whether you don't yet have a clue, I can help you achieve your dreams.

We are all on this journey together. Michelle Obama said it best, "I am becoming, and I have a story that I want to share." So, let's open our hearts and minds through my journey and experience. Allow God to fill your mind with your desires, to reveal your innate gift and talent, and to establish a blueprint to reach your goals. His ultimate purpose is for our lives to prosper.

Now, Let's Get at It!

CHAPTER 1
Identify Your Gift

Do you know what your God-given talent is? Before answering this question, let's explore what a God-given talent is. A God-given talent is a gift that is given to everyone when they are born. There is nothing you have to do to earn it. Some people receive multiple gifts, but everyone definitely receives at least one. We all have talents and gifts, some of those talents are exercised, some of those you can train to become better, and then there are some talents that come naturally, and they are God's given talent.

Parents can detect talents within their children at a very young age. There are some kids with artistic bents—they can draw, paint, and are very creative in arts and crafts. There are others who are exceptionally fast, athletic, and excel in all competitive sports and games. And then there are those people who are considered prodigies or savants, the child with a photographic memory or the one who can play a song just by hearing it once.

Autistic artist Stephen Wiltshire can sketch entire city landscapes solely from memory. Beyonce's dad released clips of her as a little girl performing. She was not shy, and she projected stage presence at a very young age. He knew that she was destined to be a star.

Likewise, my mom knew I had a gift for doing hair. One Christmas, I begged for a Barbie head bust, and styling her hair became one of my favorite past times. As I grew older, my mom saw a natural talent, a talent that I didn't have to work hard at doing because it was intrinsically inside me. All I knew was that I was simply doing hair.

I grew up with strong family values. My grandfather was born and raised on the island of the Bahamas and moved to the United States, where he started a successful family business from scratch. I was given a direct example from my grandfather about the struggle and the importance of persevering. My family's business success afforded me opportunities at a very young age. My grandmother was a housewife with very little education. She had a strong belief in God and love for her family. My grandmother taught me about the power of love, faith, prayer, and trusting in God.

I started doing hair in high school but a small disclosure—I had a Jerri curl. Outside of me getting one side cut shorter like Salt N Peppa, that was the extent of my hair fashion. I wasn't allowed to get hair color or shave one side. In comparison to my friends, I was the one with the most hair restrictions, but what no one could take from me was my penchant for knowing the latest hair trends and styles, so my cousins and my friend's hair always stayed fly.

I'm originally from Miami, Florida, a melting pot of different nationalities and cultures. I wasn't raised in a black or white community. My neighborhood was an assemblage of Cubans, Haitians, Jamaicans, Whites, and African Americans, so everyone had different textures of hair and their own unique style. At the time, I did not realize the benefits of mastering so many varying textures and combatting the Miami heat and humidity, which can play havoc on all hair types.

Unbeknown to me, this was just the beginning of the road to my future. The experience perpetuated and prepared me for the outcry for more diversification with black hair, that same outcry that black Hollywood often complains about today.

Growing up in a family that owned and operated their own business and watching my older cousin go off to college, motivated me to do the same. At the time, my cousin and I were the only two grandkids, so college, as the next step, was all I knew. I lived high school to the fullest. Although I wasn't involved in any sports, I was involved in social clubs. My counselors selected me to attend college tours, which further fed my desire to go to college.

I wasn't the best test taker, but I maintained good grades throughout the year. I applied to five colleges, and I got accepted into three. After graduating from high school, I attended Morris Brown College in Atlanta, Georgia. Morris Brown was a blessing for me. The historically black college gave me and other students the opportunity to receive a quality higher education.

My confidence as a young adult derived from being away from my family. I remember my family dropping me off at college, and I had to participate in parent-student orientations. There were student advisors everywhere, assisting students through the enrollment process. After a week, my parents returned home, the smoke had cleared, and reality settled in. This change forced me to plant my feet on solid ground. I remembered everything that was instilled in me from a young age and knew that God had not given me the spirit of fear, but love, strength, and a sound mind.

I left the state of Florida with absolutely no idea of what I wanted to major in. I was my friends' problem solver, so I thought psychology would be an excellent major. I sat with financial aid and academic advisors to determine the right classes to take for my major, even though I wasn't one hundred percent certain. People, relationships, personalities were my interests. I was always friendly and got along with people, and through my experience, I had to acclimate to a roommate and a whole new set of new people.

My first year at Morris Brown College, I took all my prep courses, and I did well. I felt I was on my way. My second year, I started the beginning courses of psychology and had no idea the courses would start at the beginning of humanity and with the anatomy of the brain. I remember sitting in my class, thinking, "What in the world did I sign up for?" This is not what I thought this subject was about.

I recalled the story of a young girl that baked cakes. She learned how to bake cakes from her grandmother. The girl was at her grandmother's hip as every cake order was placed. Once her grandmother passed, this girl was the appointed cake baker. She baked cakes for all the family events, and eventually, people and organizations placed orders from someone who started at her grandmother's hip and was now one of the best cake makers in her town. Social media and technology took off, and it was time for her to "Build her Brand." She opened a bakery and had a grand opening, but instead of cakes, she decided to bake an assortment of gourmet cookies. Her gift was baking, and her God-given talent was baking cakes; yet, she chose not to highlight her God-given gift when she debuted her bakery. When recognizing your God-given gift, be mindful not to allow social media to compromise what you are already equipped with. This story encouraged me to seek and recognize my God-given gift.

I immediately determined psychology was not what I had in mind. Or perhaps, not what God had in mind for me. With time being money and money being time, I had to think and think fast. Going back to what was familiar, I decided on business administration as my major. I was on track as a college student. Not knowing what I was going to do after college and figuring out what company I wanted to work for or what business I wanted to start was not on my radar. As I strove to meet my academic pursuits, I was also an active student with a huge personality, and I was involved in a variety of college activities, including business club. I also served as a residential assistant while maintaining a 3.1 GPA.

My junior year at Morris Brown College is when I truly exercised my gift. By then, college life had settled in, and I had acclimated to the new city and everything that came with it. Homecoming was poppin', the parties were lit, and the boys were choosing. Still not recognizing my talent, I directed my focus on my college courses. I styled hair because one of my friends was a cheerleader, another one was a four-year-scholarship recipient, the other had been named Miss Congeniality, and the last one was from the islands, so she had to bring her island swag. We thought we were the most dop chicks on campus; however, there was a price to pay for all that swag and guess who was the designated hairstylist... Me!

I started receiving a lot of buzz surrounding my ability to do hair, but unfortunately, hair wasn't my strongest desire, and I didn't have the confidence to consider myself a hairstylist. There were a few special friends that would ask me to do their hair, which led me to have about five Kmart dryers being lined up in my college apartment. My roommate Jenitha was my shampoo assistant at the sink in the kitchen, and the maintenance man knew my friends and me on a first-name basis. Every Saturday morning, he had to come and reset the circuit breaker because we inevitably blew the fuses left and right.

My senior year at Morris Brown College quickly propelled me toward graduation, and I was forced to make next-level decisions. I applied and got accepted into graduate school at Clark Atlanta

University, majoring in Public Administration. Human Resources was my concentration as I still had an urge to work with people and diverse personalities while utilizing a business degree.

At the time, this major was the best formula. On my path to pursuing my dreams, graduate school was part-time. I had to hit the workforce. Student loans accumulated, grad school courses were extremely challenging, and the bill creditors were knocking at my door every thirty days. My mom had completed her obligation and more by putting me through high school and undergrad. The decision for me to attend grad school was not a part of my single mom's financial plan.

I was at a crossroads and forced to make some tough decisions. What could I do? Could I do hair, nails? Should I start a prepaid legal business, or should I start selling Amway?

All these questions swirled in my mind regarding my next phase in life. Multi-marketing business seemed to be the most attainable business without having a lot of capital, and it seemed to be a business I could afford. I was still doing hair on the side, but one day, out of nowhere, I received an epiphany to pursue hair as my main career. The problem was, I had to go back to my mom to explain my plan on leaving grad school to go to cosmetology school—two totally different career paths and directions.

I enrolled in hair school and hit the ground running. This was the hardest decision I had to make to date because there was no financial aid, and there was little financial support from my family. There were bills, and I had to mature, stay focused, and stay true to the decision that I made.

There were times when fear crept in. Fear is a strong emotion that instinctively alerts us of danger. Fear can also cause you to create images, boundaries, and a complete story based on the emotions that were formed counter to what is real. Fear is the opposite of faith. It is impossible to walk in faith and walk in fear at the same time. These two actions are on the opposite side of the pendulum. To do both at the same time will cancel out the score, causing neutral or no results.

Insecurity is the polar opposite of confidence. Insecurity is birthed from many things, like what you were taught when you were younger, what and who is or isn't shaping your mindset set today, and how your life is fueled, as well as people, places, and things.

These are all major factors in the progression of our life, and at this time, insecurities were at an all-time high for me. All my peers were landing positions with Fortune 500 companies. They were starting their own businesses, entering into higher education, and I was going to…hair school!

As I said earlier, hair was never my desired goal, fear, and insecurity overshadowed me from receiving and acknowledging my God-given talent. I was afraid, and I thought I wasn't the hair or makeup girl. Hairstylists are known to be very posh, stylish, and trendy. My image of a hairstylist was one who was always on point. I was never the person who was overly concerned about the projection of my image, but I always carried myself in a conservative, stylish fashion. However, this was not my everyday focal point.

After graduating from hair school, my dear friend Merhet, who believed in me from the very beginning, kept telling me about her hairstylist needing an assistant. I reached out to her and was immediately hired.

This was a small, swanky salon in downtown Atlanta. What my girlfriend failed to tell me was the number of clients serviced in the salon. There were celebrities and fashion-forward women who frequented the salon.

So, here I am with the college graduate mentality, fresh out of beauty school being placed in one of the hottest, upscale salons in Atlanta. Talk about a fish out of water!

With strong feelings of not belonging, insecurities about being talented enough to handle the high-skill level of the salon, this was a pivotal point in which my faith had to be more present than my fear.

My mom's advice was that I couldn't afford to buy a whole new wardrobe or upgrade the material things in my life. I had to make sure I was neat—kept my hair done and applied makeup every day. She encouraged me to take my smile, my positive energy, and go to work and do my very best. At this point, I realized God had placed me in a situation in which He saw fit for my life. It was a place that forced me to exercise my faith.

However, in my mind, I did not belong. I encouraged myself daily. The person who I am and the skill sets that I brought to the table invoked a presence in which the clients trusted me, and a confidence I knew was not previously part of my personality, but further gained the trust of the clients. This was my God-given talent. And I finally took hold of this in my spirit.

After being an assistant for about a year, the experience equipped me with the confidence to take on my own clients. I moved to Divine Perfections Hair Salon, a salon that was still high-end, and which included my targeted clientele. However, this salon was more family-oriented, it was a mix of stylists and barbers, and the clients and stylists were down to earth and unpretentious.

This was when I developed my plan and created goals. There are many times when we are placed in positions and situations that will foster development in our lives. Centering ourselves and allowing God to move in our lives is a vital point of growth.

At this salon, the booth rent was $175 a week. I only came to the salon with a few clients, so meeting that goal under those conditions was impossible. The owner, Barbara Lewis, to this day, holds a place dear in my heart. She believed in me, encouraged me, and was placed in my life to shape and mold me into an independent hairstylist. She saw the effort I used in servicing my clients and saw the effort I used in recruiting clients. She gave me an offer to pay only $50 for a month. although, after the first month, the fee increased to $100, which we will revisit later.

A grateful heart and determination caused me to work my tail off. I was presented with an opportunity that many don't get, so I was on a mission to deliver. And I did!

It took about three months for me to acquire consistent clients. One Saturday afternoon, I pulled her to the side and handed her my booth rent of $175. I thanked her for assisting me while I built my clientele. I was finally at a place where I felt comfortable giving her my full booth rent.

Integrity is something that should be incorporated into your journey. Integrity is a quality that enforces longevity. Sadly, everyone doesn't operate under the law of integrity, but honesty and morals set you in a lane where you can detect other people that are honest and moral. As you continue on your journey, integrity will stand out like flashing lights.

Why is it important to surround yourself with like-minded people? Society and socialism have changed the measure of true success, morals, and values. Social media can be a very delusional tool, causing you to keep raising your bar. It will have you believing that you're going nowhere fast. Social media is a blessing and a curse at the same time. A blessing in the fact that every answer, every need is found at the snap of a finger. What took three years to accomplish years ago, can take three months with the use of social media and technology. The information that is instantly accessible on social media is mind-blowing.

The downfall or curse with social media is that you can create a whole new you through these platforms. You can live the life you always dreamed of living. You can also be the size, shape, and skin color you want through technology, but as soon as you log off, you are forced to live your truth. A core support group, true friends, organizations, like-minded people will assist you in truthfully navigating your path.

People, places, and things are three things that I evaluate every six months. If the people, the places, and the things you associate with are not an asset, then they are a liability. A liability isn't necessarily a bad thing but know that it is not adding value either. If you are on a journey to success, adding value is critical to your path. Take a moment to examine the last six months of your life.

Below is a chart to get you started.

> PEOPLE (Scroll through your cell phone and see who is taking most of your time)
>
> PLACES (Monitor places and time spent outside of work)
>
> THINGS (Check bank statements to get an accurate estimate of where your money is being spent)

Additionally, take time to ponder and answer the following questions. Complete this activity to help zero in on your focus as to what your God-given talent in life is.

My grandfather McDonald Johnson Sr.

30 years of friendship

Journal Activity

✱ What is something you were told all your life that you were good at, whether from family, teachers, or coaches?

_____

_____

_____

_____

✱ What is that one thing, without any pressure, or any help that you do that always garners great results?

_____

_____

_____

_____

✱ Is there a burning desire for something that keeps nudging your spirit? (Whether it's an idea, a patent, a business, or a concept that will not go away).

_____

_____

_____

_____

✱ If you were given a million dollars and someone told you that you don't ever have to work again, what would be your interest?

_____

_____

_____

_____

★ Write down your goal.? This is perhaps what you want to do to reach where you see yourself.

_____

_____

_____

_____

★ Write down your dream goal.? This is going to require a little faith.

_____

_____

_____

_____

CHAPTER 2

A Position To Win

Now that you know what God has placed in you, it's time to start using it. On a mission to be the best in my field, having thrown in the towel on a quest to take on entrepreneurship, seeking information, asking questions, not knowing anyone in route to my career path, I was determined not to fail.

At the time, the internet wasn't in existence, so there was no means of technology that connected individuals socially or educationally. Resources were limited. I felt like I was traveling from New York to California with no map or GPS, trying to figure out a path without a plan.

I contacted a publication called Oz magazine, which is a publication that focuses on television, film, print, and news media industries. I have no idea who the gentleman was that gave me the nugget of information that jump-started my career. I recall asking him if he knew or could recommend anyone or any organization that I could affiliate within the hair industry. He specifically asked me what my goal was? I couldn't completely answer the question. My response was vague and all over the place. He then advised me to look at my craft, which was hairstyling in its entirety. He said hair was affiliated with everything. If a person is involved, a hairstylist was needed—TV, film, commercials, politicians, doctors, lawyers, fashion, print—a hairstylist is required for every professional.

At the time, vision board parties had not yet been created, but what it was in existence were dream boards. The gentleman at Oz magazine told me to create a dream board, write my full name, and draw a line or subtitle for everything I wanted to do in my field.

By executing this suggestion, I created a road map that broke down my entire career path. I began by taking each subtopic and specific task one at a time. This is a simple but powerful exercise that kept me focused. After researching each title, I was able to eliminate what I was no longer interested in and take out distractions that were not in sync with my path.

Twenty years later, by the grace of God, what I have accomplished is surpassing everything that was on my vision board and anything that I have ever dreamed of.

Changing careers, moving in another direction, being perplexed by a decision you've made, and being unfamiliar on how to navigate in that decision can cause an individual to become paralyzed. Once I decided that I was completely dedicated to taking the hair path, it compelled me to think differently. Standing on that decision, not looking back and declaring, "All of you, Lord and none of me," led and directed me to walk into new territory. I'm walking at a level that is beyond my control because I'm not an expert in this field. I was a rookie, a fish out of water with a gut feeling in my spirit that I had made the right decision.

Strong desires of wanting something and seeing myself on that level but having little knowledge to take action, left me feeling like a dreamer. To desire means to have a strong feeling of wanting to have something or wishing for something to happen. It's a sense of longing and hoping for an outcome.

Being transparent with myself and pinpointing this part of my personality forced me to get connected with like-minded people. The first organization I became affiliated with was Women in Film Atlanta. Connecting with this organization broadened my horizons. It was the light switch to the world of television and film.

Working and striving on the day-to-day grind in the hair salon, servicing twenty-five to thirty clients a week, left me no options, but to focus on my clients. Staying educated with the latest color formulations and keeping up with the hottest trends has always been the key to acquiring and maintaining clientele. My corporate clients' primary hair goals were healthy hair and a chic cut; however, my fly girls wanted to turn heads every time they left the salon. My clients constantly pushed the limits of my creativity, and I loved it.

There was one client, in particular, Lisa Johnson, who received my contact information from a magazine in Los Angeles. She moved to Atlanta, made an appointment, and the chemistry between her and me was magical. West Coast and the south are two totally different worlds relating when it comes to fashion and hairstyling. After a few visits, consulting and communicating, we were on one accord with her hair styling needs. We formed a relationship, and I discovered she was a TV and Film producer. She explained to me what the role of a producer was and also discussed the different personalities that excelled in the TV television and Film industry.

Television and film was the direction I was moving toward, so I was excited to get some insight on what I was about to embark upon. The blow came when one day, she received a color treatment. This was a long process, so there was plenty of time for her and me to get into an intense conversation. (Thank God for having people around me that can give me their honest opinion and thank God I have a personality that is open to receive constructive criticism). My personality was too passive, so she proceeded to tell me I needed to become stronger to survive in the TV and Film industry. I was taken by her words because I was already successfully servicing a full clientele, and life was great.

"What do you mean I'm too passive?" I asked. She replied, "Tracey, this business is treacherous. You must possess a certain amount of confidence when entering on day one to all moving parts of this business because if you don't have it, you will get eaten by the sharks."

Luckily for me, she did not leave me with just her opinion; she offered me a suggestion, and that was for me to take an acting class. Why would I ever do that? I want to be behind the scenes. I've never had a desire to become an actress. After she explained her reasoning, however, I found a local acting company and signed up for the class.

The decision at the time was made out of respect and trust of someone that has traveled the road I wanted to travel. The purpose of me taking the acting class was for me to activate and strategically learn about another side of my personality that lay dormant within me. It forced me to pull out a side that I clearly felt wasn't me because I never had a reason to tap into this side of my personality.

Sometimes in life, we go through challenges, failures, disappointments, not knowing that God knows and sees it all. Sometimes we are faced with things in order to help us build character. We have to build strength in unknown areas to equip us for what lies ahead. To walk in the gym and start lifting major weights without warming up or conditioning yourself can cause major damage.

There are certain machines or techniques to tone specific areas of your body, so over a period of time, you will have your desired shape. Your body will be proportioned, and you will feel incredible. By not taking small steps to build muscle in weak areas, you may not attain the specific condition in certain areas to create balance for an overall look. Beyoncé versus Sasha Fierce, Tip versus TI. Who is your alter ego? That alter ego takes you out of your everyday element. Sometimes, that alter ego is the one that creates the stardom. Do you have one buried deep inside that you've ever thought about?

The beginning warm-up was intense for me because it was uncomfortable to make weird sounds, and dance around people I did not know. There were exercises in the class where I had to reenact different scenes—scenes that completely took me out of my element. I realized I wasn't built tough, I endured obstacles, but immediately I know spontaneous, forced pressure was not my strength. That acting class caused me to reevaluate myself. I am very thankful that I was given that advice because it activated the alter ego inside me that was necessary to navigate in a field that was forever changing.

There's an old quote that says, "If you want to go somewhere, go. But if you want to go far, go." Social media tends to dilute experience and credentials. Branding and marketing have a way of fabricating and creating false images of people and businesses.

Networking and researching are essential for permanent growth.

Someone once told me a story about a homeless man. This man was walking down the street and saw a stone that looked quite peculiar to him. He picked the stone up and showed it to his other homeless buddies. They laughed and said, "Man, you need to throw that rock away." For some reason, he had an inclination about the stone, so he kept it. With no goals, no ambition, the homeless man cleaned and polished the stone to the best of his ability. He was very excited and took the stone back to his buddies and told them to check it out now because he felt they definitely should be able to see what he saw. Again, they laughed, saying, "Man, you still walking around with that rock? You need to throw that rock away."

Every Sunday, his sisters would meet at his mom's house, which was on the other side of town. It's had been a few years since the man went there because his mom had died. He was not only homeless, but he had no desire to be around his family. This particular Sunday, however, the man showed up at his mom's house because, in his own will, his network of family was his only option. The instinct about the rock was very strong, and the desire to return to his mother's house was unbelievable. The man's sister took the stone to the family jeweler and discovered it was a rare Egyptian stone that was appraised for over $70,000.

The moral of the story is networking is equivalent to branches on a tree, and the tree symbolizes the mind. The branches symbolize wisdom, information, companies, and people connected to your desired goal. Certainly, you don't have to connect with one particular tree to reach your goals, but in due season, and the relationship with other trees, harvest time will provide fruit and more seeds to plant, seeds that will cause you to excel in areas that would normally take years.

I was a platform artist at the Bronner Brothers Hair Show in Atlanta when I received a phone call from R&B singer Monica's management to check my availability to style her hair for television show BET 106 and Park. Monica and I had known each other for a few years, so we were not strangers. However, this was my first time being her hairstylist. The nerves were on, and the pressure was high because not only was I styling her hair for the show, but I also had to style her hair for a Hype Hair Magazine cover. Everything went well, and I thank God. I was booked for a few more dates.

Although I was five years into doing music videos, being someone's personal stylist was a totally different beast. When you don't pass a test in life, you will definitely have to take it again, and I can't stress enough how God will continue to equip you along your journey if you trust his process.

One day, Monica and I were in the salon getting ready for an event. We talked about personalities, and she made a joke about when she and I are alone in the salon. She said at those times I have a lot of personality, but as soon as we get to an event, and the lights and cameras start rolling, she notices that I draw closer and closer to a wall, and no one hears a sound out of me.

We laughed because, me shying away was not my intention; I thought I was getting out of the way. But as I delved deeper into my career, I reflected on past experiences, and I realized there is a difference between being humble and walking in with insecurities. When you know that you are exercising the talent that God has given you, you must not allow negative thoughts and insecurities to dilute the power of your gift. Your greatest asset will always be your greatest asset. If you are a beautiful person inside, it does not matter if you are dressed like a bum that day. What people see and know about you is that you are beautiful. Walk in your gift, receive it, work it, and own it.

Monica NBA Finals Singing National Anthem

STYLING BY FAITH | 43

Monica Hype Hair Magazine Cover

CHAPTER 3

Strategic Moves

This chapter discusses "Strategic moves and, in my opinion, is one of the most important chapters of this book. Strategic Moves can propel you to a position that will set you up for the rest of your career. However, it can also, if not calculated properly, cause various setbacks like the loss of time, money, and momentum.

For my millennials, this is the chapter where we will exert all of our energy into a game of chess. Our goal is to play to win and not win to play. This is the point where you have branded, marketed, and influenced everyone that you have spoken to regarding your million-dollar idea or business. However, everyone does not always make it through the next level of Shark Tank. So, we are about to fine-tune and precisely execute your moves.

For my career changers, we do not have any more time to haphazardly make strategic moves. We must make your next move - your best move. Time is of the essence, so let's do it.

And for my professional veterans, we certainly know we have too much at risk for any false moves. Calculated moves are the only moves that we are willing to take. So, let's dive in and continue to excel in this journey.

First and foremost, it is all a risk. This is business, my friend, and nothing is one hundred percent certain. Everyone appears to be an expert in their field. Social media is popular, and so many people are hosting classes and seminars. Who should we trust? Who is actually educated and experienced in their field or can be considered marketing gurus? This is the point in which you must go back to your source, return to sender, get back to the one that gave you the gift, and equipped you with the idea. God.

As I continue on this journey, I seek Him and trust Him to lead and guide me toward my next move. Intuition is a gut feeling that lays inside you. Regardless of your situation, no one can interfere with your intuition. This is a critical point in which and you have to trust it. All doors that open, are not to be walked through; all business deals that are delivered are not to be closed, and all meeting invitations are not to be accepted. This is the point where we must use wisdom like never before in making strategic moves along the path we have chosen.

Having grandparents from the islands and having an aunt who I traveled with at a young age, I lived a life as a traveler;. Purposefully traveling abroad ignited a flame that sparked a different perspective of the world. Prior to this trip, I thought it would be a good idea for me to take a crash course to learn how to speak French. as I knew most of my time would be spent in Paris. Maximizing opportunities was instilled in me in high school, and I learned the valuable lesson that once an opportunity has passed, it's over, and you rarely get to retract what you've missed. I did not want to walk in this opportunity and not receive all the knowledge I could because of a language barrier. So, preparing myself ranked high on my things-to-do list. My first stop was Germany.

"If only I knew then what I know now" is a famous quote that is often quoted many years after the experience.

My first stop was Germany. I was twenty-four when I traveled abroad, living my best life. I researched the culture before traveling and took a French class to prepare myself to the best of my ability for the opportunity. While in Germany, traveling through the city on public transportation in a foreign country and not understanding the language was very scary and also frustrating. One of the organizers of the program noticed my frustration. She purposely gave me no assistance with the intent to teach a life lesson. I panicked, not knowing where I was and having no one around me who spoke English. There was a moment of truth when she pulled me to the side and explained how she wanted to teach me the importance of learning how to navigate the city through reading pictures and signs. Every map had words, and the signs were color-coded, shaded, or had some type of shapes or objects that provided precise directions without the need of understanding the words. I began to look and read maps with a different set of eyes. I can now go anywhere in the world without knowing anyone or the language and still get to my destination.

That day was tough, I wanted to go home, and I felt like I was being mistreated, but in the broad scheme of things, my takeaway was as you're mapping out your life or if you're in a particular stage in your life, remember everything is not going to stand out. Be bold. Be patient. Look closer, zoom in on the details, because wherever you are, there is always a path to lead you to your final destination.

Following Germany, my second stop was Switzerland, and by the time we landed in Paris, I still did not know French and at times, felt like I was losing my native English language. And boy, I could only assume what they thought about me not knowing the French language.

Thank God, for me, English is a universal language. Fortunately, more people than I thought spoke English, and we were able to communicate verbally and creatively. I learned how to communicate through art, which was perfect, speaking creatively is a universal language.

My experience was empowering. I took the biggest leap of faith. This wasn't a part of anything I've had dreamed of. It's one thing to travel outside of your home country; it's another to travel outside of your home country with a purpose. The grass is always greener on the other side until you get over there.

I was always the hairstylist who received inspiration from magazines published overseas. The European cuts were always on the cutting edge. The creativity of style was different.

Overseas styles were always more stylish to me and seemed to always be on the cutting edge of fashion while breaking fashion barriers. It wasn't until I started working in the salon in Paris that I learned the same sentiments I had about overseas stylists were the exact thoughts they had about stylists from the U.S. This commonality created the best chemistry for the stylists and me in the salon. I was eager to learn their techniques and find out what was trending there, and they were, likewise, extremely excited to know what American stylists were doing as well. They were very excited and interested in American celebrities, and to show them a popular weaving technique or a hair trick from a celebrity was golden.

Working overseas was definitely not a part of my strategic plan. I never knew such an opportunity existed. I landed this opportunity by being in the right place at the right time.

My mind was set to receive and achieve greatness. I set my life purpose to win, and that energy flowed through me.

Near the beginning of my hairstylist career, as I began to build clientele in the salon, on my downtime, I took another look at my vision plan. I was always researching or trying to get information to move to the next level. There was one particular day when I was the receptionist at the salon. and three women walked in the salon and began asked asking a few questions. They wanted information about the nearest beauty school. I gave them the information, and we talked for about an hour. The conversation was primarily about them going to the beauty school to scout the top students and encourage them to apply for an opportunity as an exchange stylist. This was certainly appealing to my ears, and since I was fresh out of beauty school myself at the time, I asked if I could also apply for the position. They gave me an application and proceeded on to the beauty school. A few weeks before heading back to Paris, they contacted me. I had an interview, and I landed the position.

I'm forever grateful for the experience. I learned you have to channel your energy to succeed. Set your mind like you set your thermostat. Regardless of the changes in life, on your job, and within your plan, as long as your setting is fixed on a particular dial, it will always return to that temperature. Likewise, you can get off course, fall short of money, and not have any contacts, but as long as you keep your dial and energy set on success, it will find its way to you.

Tracey Moss exchange hairstylist Paris, France 2000

CHAPTER 4

Trust The Process

I'm very thankful for the fact that I was able to create a vision and actually accomplish almost everything that was listed on my vision board. The hurdles and hardships along the way to achieving goals are often the things that people typically don't discuss. These are the things that aren't posted on social media. The how-to-succeed classes are more appealing topics as they dive into the process and the sacrifices that are made before the victory.

Along with these sacrifices come questions. Is it worth it? Is this something that I really need to be doing now? When in the trenches of a project or goal, everything else seems easier, faster, and it also sometimes seems like the rewards are greater when other people are doing it.

When starting a goal, compare your trajectory like planting a seed. There is a lot of prep work in planting the seed that is required before you actually begin to plant. Finding the area to dig and making sure you have the best soil to initiate growth are super important. Knowing how often you need to water the area and protect it from too much sun and the elements to help stimulate growth are vital. Whatever seed you are planting, you must make sure you are knowledgeable of what part of the year or what season is best for planting. All of these questions need answers before the digging process begins. And once you plant the seed, knowing how often to water is critical because this is the initial step to determine whether or not your dream or seed will take root. You cannot see and will not see what takes place underground. You have to trust the process and be patient. Stay consistent with watering, and be in sync with outside weather conditions.

Now that the seed has taken root, it breaks ground, and you have birthed a tiny little stem—not a plant, not fruit, not a tree—just a tiny stem. Now, the work is about to really begin. It's like having a delicate newborn baby or getting all your business forms and certifications, and you aren't ready to launch your new business. There are so many factors to watch out for in the beginning to ensure your dream won't die.

The next stage is a plant or a flower—it is now at its full stage of growth. However, it still has not produced anything. A lot of time has gone by; your plant has almost died twice, the weather has been horrible, and it seems like the season is about to change. You think to yourself, what have I gotten myself into? Then you start to see fruit, and with fruit, there are seeds and a possibility to plant more seeds as your harvest begins.

Questioning decisions is a natural thing to do, but while I am in the middle of the process, I always refer back to a seed. It takes time; I won't be able to see the results immediately, but if I keep pursuing my goal, it will eventually create a harvest.

Music videos were a part of my vision board. When I created my board, there was a lot of critical thinking associated with it. During my dreaming season, there were no narratives to the story. I didn't have any answers on how I was going to achieve anything on the board. That season was just about dreaming. Think of all the things you want to do, write down all your desires, big and small. Write down things that you feel like you can achieve immediately and write down long-term goals you feel might be a little impossible to achieve.

Under the music video section, I asked the question, why? One obvious desire for music videos was celebrities, then more money, more fame, which led to other celebrities, but another reason for me was the opportunity to set trends. Again, social media, Pinterest, and Instagram were nonexistent, so music videos were the platform to creatively display my talent for high-level clients and set that trend. The creative vision is already created by the time the concept gets to the artist's glam squad—a team made up of makeup artists, stylists, and hairstylists.

The total look for the artist is a combination of ideas and thoughts from the team and at least sixty percent from the artist. It's important to conduct your research, know their label mates, and their genre of music. The last thing you want to do is not be aware of trending styles and have your client seen with the same look of another artist at the same event.

One of the coolest things with music clients is when you receive that call from a label, and they ask your rates on artist development. Artist development is different from an existing artist, whose style and look are already developed. With an existing artist, your primary goal is to continue to move fashion-forward, while staying true to the bracket that the label has established for the artist. However, when you have a client in artist development, you're in the beginning stage of their project. They just signed with a label, and now, it's time to create a superstar look. From the glam squad perspective, this is the time to showcase your artistic skills.

Working on TV and Film sets is something totally different than I have ever done and experienced, mainly because I am an IATSE 798 Union member. Becoming a union member was no easy task. I had no idea this organization even existed. This information came to me by networking and socializing with like-minded people. Being a part of a union afforded me certain protections.

There are standards and rules that must be abided by when working on a TV and Film project, and also, everyone is held responsible for following their particular union laws. When working under prescribed guidelines, the thought process is different because there is order, and with that order becomes accountability. There is a lot at stake and a lot of money involved with each show.

I discovered how I am definitely playing in a political field. My experience in TV and Film is more of a corporate feel than a freelance field, where you're walking into every project, knowing there is a ladder of hierarchy. Everyone has to answer to someone. This is not about you and your ego; this is about knowing and believing you have a gift, or you would not be here. However, you must use your skillset to carry out a vision that's far greater than you. Nothing is to be taken personally from talent to the network; you are a vessel to create artistry.

The five-year period I worked on music videos was a period for growth. This was the beginning of freelance for me. I had returned from apprenticing overseas for my first music video for Lil Bow Wow's "Ghetto Girls." I worked with more than twenty-five artists during the time. A Whitney Houston music video was one of the highest-profile videos I'd ever worked on. The iconic Whitney Houston! In my mind, had I truly arrived. I have always been a fan. I loved her, her music, and her image from day one, and to be in close proximity to such a talented superstar, I was in awe the whole day. Out of all videos to date, that is my most memorable.

50 Cent's "In The Club" was another memorable music video. I remember calling my cousin and asking him if he knew of a rapper named 50 Cent. He said, "Yes. He's a raw

underground mixtape artist." I replied, "Well, I just got the call to be a part of the hairstyling team to create his music video." My cousin said, "Word! That's big?" We traveled to LA and did the music video, having no idea this was going to be the hottest song for the year.

Atlanta artists were on fire at the time and in heavy rotation. To watch Tip progress into "TI" was very rewarding. I was a hairstylist on one of his first videos, "I'm Serious." He was young and blowing up after being released from a record label, and he had a point to prove. And Mr. Harris has been proving his point ever since.

I also worked on music videos for Outkast and Goodie Mob. The rapper T Mo Goodie and I were college classmates and great friends. He also became a hair client and faithfully got his hair braided. So, to circle back around to braiding his hair for award shows and his music videos were moments I will forever cherish. Mob Deep, Busta Rhymes, Ashanti, Nelly, Fabulous, Cash Money, Lil John, Lil Scrappy, and hometown JT Money were a host of music videos that I can proudly say; I was a part of creating.

I had mentioned earlier that working on a music video with Whitney Houston had been my indicator that I arrived.

However, I would have to say that the MTV VMA award show in New York City was the pinnacle of my success.

This was a very exciting time in my journey. The city was on fire, and that was my first time attending the VMA awards show.

The venue was packed any and every celebrity you could think of was in attendance.

I was one of the hairstylists for P. Diddy's performance. Working with P. Diddy and the Bad Boy family was a learning experience. There was a level of excellence that he required from every person associated with whatever project he was working on. P. Diddy is very involved with the process of his success. The energy was up, the pressure was on, and the team that was chosen to carry out his vision was responsible for delivering a superior performance.

Although teamwork makes the dream work, I felt compelled to make sure every hairstyle I created was created with honor and dignity. That was the energy that was in the building. Not only was there a sense of natural competition to have the best performance of the night, but also an individual energy to do your very best.

Right before it was time for the team to take the stage, Diddy said a speech and a prayer. This speech made a lasting impression with me. He told the team to go out and perform like it was their last performance—nothing was guaranteed. "The audience does not have to clap for you; you did not have to make it to this level. Don't get to this point and do yourself an injustice by giving a mediocre performance. Leave it on the dance floor. Let's go out and create magic!"

He did not only leave it there, but he also said a dynamic prayer that summoned God to work through each individual. He invoked God into the whole performance. "God, we have prepared ourselves to the best of our ability. Now anoint this performance."

Please understand how powerful those five minutes were. That moment has impacted my life ever since. There are a million people doing the same thing you're doing and have the same gift you have. No one is obligated to support you, give you information, assist, or even talk to you. Treat every step like it's the end; work with pride and dignity. Walk with confidence and create magic every step of the way.

Every video, award show, artist, and experience thus far has sharpened my skills and boosted my confidence. Staying grateful and positive is the key to propel transparency, which allowed me to learn from my mistakes. Constructive criticism was viewed from the eyes of growth and not from the eyes of failure. Iron sharpens iron. To know and appreciate the veterans around you, to value the pioneers that paved the way for you will bolster a force that will cause people to want you to be a part of their team or want to do business with your company. I embrace my journey, good and bad.

When I worked on my first television show, Tyler Perry's "Meet the Browns," I was acquainted with how productions operated, and I was also aware of how important time was. What I wasn't totally prepared for was creating characters. The intricate details that take place when creating characters were very interesting. It didn't have anything to do with fashion or a trend; it was simply artistically delivering a story.

There are many layers to television and film, but my experiences equipped me for the journey. There are times when you find yourself in a situation that is dark, and sometimes, things aren't clear until you get in another situation, and you realize that all the trials you endured strengthened you for the road ahead.

STYLING BY FAITH | 63

Tracey Moss and T-Mo Goodie of rap group Goodie Mob

64 | TRACEY MOSS

Tracey Moss and P. Diddy backstage of MTV VMA awards

CHAPTER 5

Take A Leap

Owning a salon was a part of my ultimate vision for my career.

Having a business administration degree, taking courses in Human Resources, and also exercising my gift from God, salon ownership was a perfect fit. The question that was always a mystery was when and how was I going to take on this new venture. Opening a salon, restaurant, or a major business is something you never feel prepared for when it comes to having enough capital, or if you do, there is professional preparation involved.

Yes, it was something that I eventually wanted to achieve, but I did not know the logistics or execution of this particular business adventure. I was a booth renter in a successful salon in downtown Atlanta for about five years. I was currently servicing a full clientele, and I was also freelancing full time with music videos. The owner of the salon approached me with an opportunity to become a part of ownership. There was so much thought in my decision because much is given and much is required.

During those years, millennials weren't born yet, so my generation did not take on the world and everything else that came with it, there were some critical thinking involved.

What inspired me to embark upon this opportunity was the fact that it was three of us. Three women that were totally different, who all had entrepreneurial spirits, and we all were talented and professional. It was a unique blend of our strengths and weaknesses, but the balance that was developed, and the partnership was special.

Relationships, my friends, are the key to success. Yes, you can conquer the world, but without the congress, the senate, and the people, the president is made powerless. It takes a team regardless of what field or whatever profession you decide to choose.

The process of becoming an entrepreneur changes your way of thinking and your mindset. The moment monetary deposits, sacrifices, and late nights become a reality, a standard of succeeding is set. In the beginning, we were like that seed planted in the ground. We moved the salon to a new location., there was only a three-month grace period to build out the new location in which it was a total transformation from a blank canvas. Branding and marketing were required, a grand opening was in process, and all of this had to be achieved under a certain budget. It was not easy; however, contracts were signed, and the clock was ticking. The final weeks of completion, the grimy, dirty part was over, the salon was looking beautiful. We were getting prepared for the grand opening, there was still a sense of pressure, but the feeling of relief was present. The grand opening included a live, band, DJ, and wine., the block was on fire, family, friends, and clients were all in support. I felt like a boss. We did it; I completed my part and my task, what an awesome accomplishment.

From a young girl, I saw the extreme intensity of the amount of work my grandfather poured into the family business. My grandfather was the CEO of the company, but my mother, however, was the office manager, the filed representatives, and also the public face of the company.

She started in the business at thirteen, I was born when she was seventeen, so I grew up hand and hand with my grandfather and my mom sacrificing, and all while staying committed to the company.

The life lessons that I took away from growing up having a family business was definitely not the monetary things. It was the sacred lessons taught at the dinner table or the intense conversation on the way to and from a meeting. My grandfather came from the islands with a third-grade education; it was a special amount of dedication that I witnessed. Integrity was perhaps was the one thing that stuck close to me.

My grandfather was faithful to his employers and his employees. I can return to my city today, and there are men in the community who will embrace me as if I'm still that little girl who was up at 6 a.m., passing out coffee and breakfast with my grandmother to my grandfather's laborers.

My grandfather did not believe in burning any bridges; he valued his relationships and his opportunities. The commitment he had toward the community was unbelievable.

My mom, on the other hand, was in her early twenties, running her father's business like it was her own. My mom devoted her life to the company, which is a huge statement, and to date, my mom has displayed a level of commitment to my life and success with constant reassurance of what it takes to balance a successful business and family. These conversations and priceless memories will be cherished forever.

Hard work, appreciation, and sacrifices are not terms that I adapted when I got older; these adjectives were instilled in my life. No one is obligated to do a thing for you. Be grateful, thankful, appreciative, honest, and, most importantly, live with integrity; it will take you a long way.

Catching flights, attending events with clients, happy hour, concerts, and owning a salon is like stopping at a red light. They are two totally different entities, it's certainly called freelance for a reason. Freelance is based on no restrictions; the boundaries are limitless.

Owning and operating a salon for me was a challenge. Yes, I have a business administration degree, but I was accustomed to navigating through life the way I wanted to. My clients were a priority, but I was still in control of my schedule. Salon ownership takes full control of your free will. I was forced to revamp priorities, finances, time, and my mindset.

The main characteristics that laid dormant in my life were imperative to developing were leadership potential. When the salon has ten to fifteen employees, and you are one of the faces of the establishment. Owners are constantly diffusing in-salon issues; stylists are looking for advice to build clientele, the air conditioner is broken, the water is running cold, and leadership skills are mandatory.

Enhancing leadership skills has changed the scope of my brand and me. Operating a salon evoked a strength that changed my perception of myself. I made it; I was a successful operator and owner of a hair salon. God, I thank you.

Every stylist has a specialty, whether its hair cutting, hair coloring, hair weaving, or natural hair, etc. I have a pretty diverse hand; I am skilled in all areas, but I developed a reputation for hair cutting, most of my clients were professional and trendy.

The salon itself attracted stylish influential women, and we kept a squad of trendsetters. Outside of my educators, women that worked in the medical field, models, and college students were the daredevils. They weren't afraid of anything, they kept me on my toes, and I kept them popping.

Johnetta Cole, former president of Spelman College, was a jewel that I was blessed to be able to serve on a secret Sunday. She was transitioning from Atlanta to Washington DC to become the director of the Smithsonian Institution National Museum of African American Art. Mrs. Cole is royal sophistication at its finest; her energy and presence were amazing.

Kim Fields was also a client where I had the opportunity to color her hair. I did not know what to expect from Mrs. Cole; all I knew was I've been a fan since the Facts of Life.

I was leaving the salon one day when I got a call asking if I had space to take one more client. In walked David and Tamela Mann. They were down to earth and a joy to be around. David had us all cracking up.

Many people have negative stories working with different people and many problems with having multiple owners. Some of the obvious reasons are egos', too many chiefs and not enough Indians play a major factor in the pitfall of a relationship in a partnership. My experience, I must say, was different; we had a unique relationship. Outside of the business, I build to solid friendships in which turned into family. Not only were my business partners great hairstylists, but Deaundra Metzger and Tamika Dixon were both driven women. When you go to seminars or read blogs that tell you to surround yourself around like minds and successful people, they were that type.

Sometimes you are at a point in your life in which certain things don't pertain to you. You're not interested or so disconnected from a thing because that's not your lane at the time. For me, I was single—well dating, or let's say having fun—and Dede and Tameka were mothers. God gave me a living example on how to successfully rear kids and run a successful business. They were both happily married, so to witness the balance of marriage, kids, and a striving business was priceless.

At the time we were in the trenches, we all were young and moving and never realized that once the business dissolves, God was perfectly designing a lifelong relationship. I had no idea years later how those reflections of my life would become so vital.

The puzzle of life is not always about what our minds can compute. Once we incorporate God in every area of our lives, trusting the process is key.

Reflecting on those years, reminiscing on those priceless moments, the salon has come and gone, but gaining two beautiful sisters is the part of that experience that was not on my vision board. I had things, desires, and wants, and only God knew the essence of how important these two women were going to be in my life. Trust the process, friends!

Opportunities are often presented when you are striving in your lane of success; it's called the law of attraction. When a partnership idea is presented to you or your business plan is formulated with a partner, the safest approach proceeding is to be aware of the pros and cons of a partnership. Statistics show a partnership being successful is less than 70 seventy percent.

Millennials considering a partnership may not be a bad idea simply because of the way you view goals and success. Millennials tend to have million-dollar ideas and also have a business plan that could fill the shoes of a corporation. You think big and expect fast results. This is not a negative attribute to process, but what makes it negative is when an individual doesn't take ownership of knowing themselves and recognizing this type of mindset.

Choosing a partner requires first being honest with who you are, your style of thinking, and accepting your strengths and weaknesses. Once contracts are signed, this is not the time to figure out your personal or business style.

A benefit to partnerships and a secret weapon for my millennial is splitting obligations because if you are not pursuing other businesses and ideas, they are coming.

Setting boundaries during this time is essential, and recognizing who should be the leader is also important for partnerships to strive. Appointing a leader does not mean the other person is weak or incompetent; it just means the leader is stronger in execution.

Visionary skills, understanding our commitment to our assignments, and strong communication skills are key to our success. It's imperative to hire an attorney to create the contract and prepare an exit strategy, and to consult with a tax accountant to illuminate any personal opinions in regards to facts.

A fifteen-year salon veteran connected with two other fifteen-year salon veterans was like a well-blended mix of oil and water. When I say oil and water, I'm referring to the fact that we all were successful professionals that were used to managing our own careers. Although we got along perfectly, we all had three very different personalities. We all seemed to have three totally different ideas when it came to solving issues. Respect and honor were a part of our DNA, which is how we were able to have effective communication while addressing our differences.

The point I want you all to receive is my obstacle did not come through the form of my partners; my obstacle came by coming face to face with myself. Self-control, learning how to get a point across without showing emotions. Standing firm on what you believe and your opinion while maintaining effective communication skills.

Co-owner obstacles grew bigger and bigger when I could not figure out how to control emotions while operating in my truth. Every level in this path of success is different; we will never be the same person we were in high school. Life is not designed like that. Maturing and respectfully speaking your truth is a major component in being a partner of any sort.

Your voice is important, and when we stand in our own way because we can't articulate what we're thinking and feeling, it's an injustice to ourselves and others. The opportunity would have never been presented or created if your personality or skill set spoke otherwise. Handle every situation with dignity and honor.

There is a substantial difference in working as a hairstylist in someone else's salon and working as a hairstylist in a salon you co-own. As a hairstylist working in someone's salon, the mindset is different. There is a level of freedom in which you're in control of your progress. There are salon rules that have to be followed and also quotas that have to be met, but there isn't a true sense of obligations.

Once my title changed from hairstylist to co-owner, it was literally an immediate difference. My freedom as a hairstylist was instantly taken up a level. To sum up, that feeling was called accountability. The roles changed, the responsibility grew overnight; my mindset was completely different because I was no longer responsible for just paying booth rent and leaving for the night.

My commitment and obligations were now my first priority. At the time, I felt the pressure. I also felt the creative freedom of just being a hairstylist suppressed; the skill set was there because hairstyling is my God-given talent; however, the responsibility of the ownership overshadowed the art.

Many times, during an experience, the lesson is not recognized until we are out of the situation. My focus was on maintaining and obtaining a successful business, not realizing that this experience added value to me as a person and a hairstylist. The knowledge I gained as a business owner when it came to finances, making decisions based on profit and loss, business strategies, and budgeting changed not only the scope of myself being a hairstylist but myself as a person.

Closing the business was forced upon us; our decision to dissolve the business wasn't because it wasn't successful. The building was getting demolished due to revamping the area. The salon was located in a prime central location in downtown Atlanta. Unfortunately, there was not enough notice to relocate, so there were some tough decisions that needed to be made immediately.

As a group, there were some options that had been brought to the table, but for me, I was at a crossroads. This point in my life brought on much sadness, my emotions ran high. I was fearful, felt that I was incompetent, and experienced separation anxiety. The force that we had as a team caused me to have doubts. I questioned whether I would still have sustainability.

This was a very dark time for me. Mentally, I was operating, and decisions were made as a team for the last eight years of my life. It felt like a divorce; the thought of the shared responsibility and the power of the team being dissolved put me in a sad place.

Soul searching and finding peace was an essential part of my decision-making. Meditating, seeking wisdom, and answers from God, and patiently waiting to receive an answer while staying positive, helped me through this sensitive point in my life. And my answer did not come on a piece of paper in my mail. My answer came through peace. The anxiety was removed, the fears were lifted, things started to make sense, and I was no longer at the forefront of my life, peace was the key to my movement.

My last day at the salon was bittersweet. I was detaching myself from a relationship that had blossomed throughout twelve years. There were a lot of memories, laughs, and love that were being separated. Over a twelve-year span, we had all grown on so many levels. I've watched their kids grow up, and the salon family was my new normal. The last day at the salon was a true solidification that it was officially over.

However, parallel to the uneasy feeling, I was also equally very proud of myself. I felt like against all the odds, a choice was made, and I was boldly walking into my decision. The accomplishment that I received out of those twelve years it didn't have anything to do with hair, relationships, or any accolades. It was about the strength that I found in believing in myself.

Within this process, I discovered the power of locating inner peace within and have come to the realization that in the midst of peace, lies the power.

Crystal clear sight, hearing, and the ability to make sound decisions in that still moment are priceless. I have received confidence in knowing the importance of exercising strength and taking responsibility for trusting and honoring my truth.

Because of this revelation, the weight was lifted, which caused me to walk with dignity, and while knowing my assignment was completed. Making and following through with a tough decision was the lesson that has promoted my entire life.

Tracey Moss, Tamika Dixon & Deaundra Metzger
Owners
360° Salon

STYLING BY FAITH | 81

David and Tamela MANN

CHAPTER 6

Get Connected

In previous chapters, I mentioned the importance of having a clear vision and attainable goals before entering into a business venture. Spending time on strategic planning and accomplishing goals is advantageous to an entrepreneur. They are equally important to add to your vision board in its transitional stage. Between each goal set and each goal achieved, there is space one needs to mentally factor in strategies and a plan. Understand how important the transitional stage will help alleviate anxiety, regulate your pace, and help you to remain balanced.

In jumping into the vast ocean of business, strategic planning is often never considered, and it requires sacrifice from your character and finances. However, it helps build you up and makes you a stronger person. How the transitional stage is handled is perhaps more important than setting and achieving goals because it sets the tone for your next goal.

Transitioning from the salon to working on set was a trying time for me. I was often exhausted, and my life felt like everything was running together. I didn't have time for myself. I juggled an extensive loyal clientele and well maintaining the demanding work schedule in television and film was not an easy task. Both jobs were a priority; my clients were my bread and butter for years, which I had a special obligation for those ladies.

TV and Film was a significant desire. It was a goal set years ago that finally came to fruition. I was determined to do both, and that is where the sacrifices of no sleep, no life became a reality.

During this time, TV and Film opportunities became more consistent. Not only was I receiving calls to work locally, but I also garnered requests to work out of town. My reputation grew exponentially, clients were excited, but I did not realize that my career in the salon was coming to an end. A call from Camille Friend, an extraordinary hairstylist and one of Marvel studios leading department heads, was the catalyst that propelled me to decide to retire from the salon. Accepting the charge from Camille to key the Miles Ahead movie in Cleveland, Ohio, changed the course of my TV and Film career.

Being a hairstylist for more than twenty years, working with product companies, and salon ownership prepared me as a stylist for television and motion pictures. To become a great production hairstylist, one must master the foundation of hairstyling, be teachable, and understand that we are helping to create characters. Working on television shows, the characters are typical ordinary looks. Many times, they could be family-based, a mystery, suspense, or reality looks. Films, on the other hand, are a different beast. The range of creativity varies from period dramas to Sci-Fi, fantasy, or horror. The level of creativity can take you out of your personal comfort zone. If a role requires a disheveled and distressed appearance, hair, makeup, and wardrobe are critical. The character cannot appear to be elegant or trendy. Everything must be toned down to deliver a compelling and believable story.

Extensive research is often dependent upon the period or the region in which the film is set. Studying your craft is vital for TV and Film. Working as a makeup artist for a 1920s movie requires different makeup that than what we see in 2019. Failure to research the era that's being filmed can cause you and your department to change the visual dynamic and creative concept of the film.

There is no 'I' in "'team'" when working on a set in any department. Everything is departmentalized when it comes to the hair department—one person alone can't make a movie. It's important to bring your A-game when you receive a call to work in a particular department. When you get an assignment, that is your time to carry out the vision. Unless you're a personal stylist for a particular actress, working as a hairstylist outside of TV and Film is your time to have full creative control to do whatever you want. It is imperative to understand that in TV and Film, the industry is a corporation, and it is political. The hair department is a slice of a bigger picture.

Freelance hairstylists, makeup artists, lash experts, and estheticians all have free will to create and manage their own business. You have full control of the direction of your business.

As a freelance hairstylist, I was fortunate to do what I've encouraged you all to do, and that is maximize my freelance freedom. Don't limit your success range because of a lack of knowledge. Network, research, and propel your career in a forever-changing business. Being complacent will stagnant your growth.

Having an umbrella of protection is necessary, as well. The International Alliance of Theatrical Stage Employees 798 (IATSE) hair and makeup was my springboard into the business. When I became a member of the East Coast chapter, it wasn't as open as it is today. It was more like a secret society. Acquiring rates and the criteria for joining was not discussed. It was a small group of members in the state of Georgia. Back then, becoming a member was a catch 22. To work on a union set, you had to be part of the union; and to join, you had to work on union sets.

A union is a body of people working together to improve their work-lives lives through collective bargaining. When you're part of a union, you collectively meet with management to discuss issues that affect you. Wages, benefits, conditions, and legal contracts are part of this discussion. Some other benefits of the union are health insurance, 401k, and pension. A freelance artist can definitely set retirement goals for themselves and their family, but being disciplined and staying on top of things that are important to retirement is vital. And networking and placing yourself in the right environments with the right people is essential to joining the union.

The television and film industry started growing in the state of Georgia as I became affiliated with the union. I began working more and more on union projects and acquired union days to work toward joining the union. My breakthrough came when I was told that theater was also an affiliate of the union. I got a referral to work on Broadway traveling shows, and they placed me in a position to consistently receive union days.

My first union project was Tyler Perry's Meet The Browns. I'll never forget the call I received from Cynthia Chapman, a twenty-five-year union member, and now the woman noted for mentoring and training me for this industry. At the time, my only focus was doing a good job. I was not thinking about the next move, money, or the union. My main concern was that an opportunity had been presented, and now it was time to handle it.

I continued to receive phone calls, and my performance led to other phone calls. After about three years, the doors of the IATSE 798 hair and makeup union opened. I had gained my days and was able to apply to join the union. I knew the criteria to join, but I did not understand the benefits until I became a member. Joining was a stress reliever. I was no longer responsible for creating TV and Film rates. Working on independent films and music videos, you are under no protection. The rates can be whatever they set, and there's probably little to no negotiations. My life became legally less complicated when I joined the union. It wasn't as stressful doing taxes, and health insurance was provided through with a group benefit, which created better rates, and retirement goals were now attainable. Being a freelance stylist is now one of my seven income goals, not my priority income. My union gig is my primary source of income.

Union projects have afforded me opportunities that have taken my resume and skillset to unforeseen levels. Being a humble, confident artist is key to success for movies. Hunger Games was one of the first movies I experienced where all the top Hollywood and Atlanta hairstylists merged and created a creative hair extravaganza. I was so excited to be part of such a creative group. White, Black,

Latino, old or young, it didn't matter which way you turned it was hairstyling at its finest. Guardians of the Galaxy, was fantasy and science fiction., as a hairstylist coming out of the salon, fantasy and science fiction was a road less traveled, it was artistic, creative, bold, and phenomenal. Bolden's Where the Music Begins film took place between 1877 and 1931. No one living today was born in 1877, and if someone randomly asked you to create an 1877 hairstyle, good luck.

Research and basic fundamental hairstyling skills are required. Fancy tools, YouTube tricks, and the latest and greatest products are out the window. Bolden was the foundation of styling natural hair, textured hair, no products, no curling iron or flat iron, and no visible hairpins. To research hairstyles for men, women, and children in the 1800s and execute them was an experience I will never forget.

The blockbuster hit, Black Panther, was one of Marvel's biggest movies, gaining worldwide acclaim. To be a part of this dynamic hair team was a memorable and special experience. An entire movie filmed with wigs and all types of natural textures was historical. It's one thing to work on a film with heavy wig work, but wig work with men while incorporating heat and sweat, forces you to execute the best products and techniques.

The Bad Boy for Life film was not complicated for a stylist. But having the opportunity to work with Will Smith and Martin Lawrence was beyond exciting. The positive energy and wisdom that Will Smith freely gave about living your best life were priceless. These are just a few testimonials of the work I've performed on set. I am beyond grateful for every TV and Film gig, big or small that I was ever blessed to be part of.

When playing a role, celebrities are sometimes caught between their personal image, the image that the world knows, and their character. Personally, I have insecurities that I try to mask, and I am not being followed by TMZ. I can only imagine what they have to deal with mentally and publicly if the character look does not compliment their best image. The judgment and ridicule can be quite harsh. Critics and fans tend to forget that the actors are playing characters. The appearance of each character is created by producers, showrunners, and network executives. For a hairstylist, makeup artist, and wardrobe stylist, sometimes it can be difficult getting celebrities to jump on the bandwagon of the corporate vision. Staying focus on delivering the story and creating a balance between the character's look and the celebrity is the name of the game.

A union set is not a freelance environment. Set life is a corporation that involves networks, production companies, unions, contracts, people that can get fined, sued, and fired. Knowing the rules, the dos and don'ts is not an option—it's a criteria.

Many people look at the finished product, the TV show, the press tour for the movie, red carpet events, the ratings, and the excitement of seeing their name in the credits. But there are millions of dollars and hard work deposited into the production of the movie long before the fun stuff begins.

Walking on set is not a playground; it is a very serious environment that everyone needs to be aware of. A few dos and don'ts that a freelance artist may not be aware of is we cannot wear open-toe shoes on set because of hazards like nails and heavy equipment. This is a hard and fast rule. From the first showtime of the day, we have six hours before lunch. Another do and don't that is very important is you always have a protocol. There's a point of contact over you, whether there is an issue or a simple question, the person over you in your department is your point of contact. Going to the producers and directors concerning a problem that could be solved in your department shows a lack of experience and causes you to get looked upon differently.

And last but not least, everyone is part of a team. I said it before; there is no "I" in "'team."' No one is freelancing. Someone hired you to carry out the desired look of the department that was established before your department was even evolved.

Women and Film annually meeting

CHAPTER 7
Bet on Yourself

If working as a freelance artist is something you seek to achieve, establish a strategic plan that matches the vision you've created. If your desire is to become a part of a union, learn the dos and don'ts of the business. These points are critical to your success and your next move.

Nothing worth having comes in a cereal box. You're going to have to work, apply yourself, and be thick-skinned. As you gain more experience and continue to put your best foot forward, your reputation will take you places you never dreamed of, and it will become the backbone of your personal brand.

We've all read that seven streams of income are the target, and with that goal in mind, it forces you to execute your personal brand to promote yourself and your accomplishments.

Personal brands are the way of the world; they are almost equal to your resume, depending on your niche and your ultimate goals. After being a veteran hairstylist, and since social media has become popular, I realized for the first twenty years that I landed jobs based on my resume. Now, many companies and celebrities judge my worth based on my social media presence. I once sat in a seminar about personal branding, and two artists were compared by experience and by the number of followers they had. According to the company, it was more beneficial to hire the person with the most followers and social media exposure. Bloggers have also moved their titles in the factual line. Some bloggers in the industry with large social media platforms have watered down experience, credentials, degrees, and licenses. I don't see this as a deterrent, but as a motivation to continue honing my skills.

While working on the film Bad Boy for Life for three months, Will Smith left a lasting impression on my life, and his words resonated with me. His energy and positive vibes impacted the cast, crew, and everyone he crossed paths with. I would like to share what I call #TheWillSmithMovement, which is: we are all in control of our minds, actions, and decisions. And being a victim is a thing of the past. We have the control to change our mind, life, perspective, health, relationship, and career.

Yes, we have all heard it before, but truly take hold of the fact that we must love ourselves more than a toxic circumstance. Allow yourself to make positive, impactful decisions and changes in your life.

My future, as I like to say, is the newest technology. You get a computer and work on it, and you'll have that computer for a few years. While working with the computer, there are always popups. Do you want to update your computer, or do you want to restart the computer? Some of your apps are outdated. The warranty for the antivirus is about to expire, and you need to extend it. You have now exceeded your data, and it's time to purchase more data. You are always given opportunities to accept it now, ask me later, or don't ask me again. However, you are constantly getting warned. Now that you have had the computer for a few years, the company has come out with two updated versions. Your computer still runs, and it still gets the job done, but it's now considered antiquated.

Our lives are like a computer; God is constantly giving us notices, warnings, pop-ups, and ideas. We are full of information. Everything we need to succeed in life is already within us. So, listen to your mind, follow your inner voice, and allow the higher being to manifest greatness in your life.

Tracey Moss

CHAPTER 8

The Power Within

"There's no business like show business" is an old saying that I now realize is true. A television show can come to your city for two months or six months. The project is filmed, then it's over until the next project. Everything about film production is fastpaced, ready or not, the show goes on.

Since being in the business for the last fifteen years, I now have new priorities, and that is balancing a family and a four-year-old little boy. Since becoming a mother, all my decisions and plans are centered around the betterment of my family and child. Being on a film set for at least fourteen hours a day, starting as early as 5 a.m., can put a strain on any situation. Trying not to neglect your family and put your kids on a schedule and get them on a routine is very challenging for TV and Film parents. I am very thankful for my village that helps me with facilitating Bryce and his little life.

You can work on a film set for six weeks to nine months, and then you're on to the next project. I've talked to so many coworkers and actors that make quality decisions on taking jobs for the betterment of their families and kids. My future plans with television and film productions are to continue to work hard, keep preparing and educating myself, and stay connected to vision makers.

At the top of this year, I was in Miami, Florida, working as a key hairstylist for Bad Boys 3. An editor called me from The Miami Herald, a local newspaper, to interview me. One of the questions was, when did you feel like you made it? My answer was a quote from Michelle Obama, "I am still becoming."

What that means in my terms is as long as I live, I am living, I am still developing and evolving. Every stage of my life has been a learning curve. I operate in complete gratefulness. I'm thankful to God for every opportunity that has been presented to me. As opportunities present themselves, I will decide whether or not it will work for the betterment of my life and my family. I know that regardless, I will be readily prepared for the opportunity.

Pursuing dreams and trying to obtain goals has put me in positions in which money was scarce, and many sacrifices had to be made. Through it all and all of the challenges, I've come to realize that I am more than enough; I have what it takes, and I am in total control of how I navigate successfully through life.

As I continue to go through this journey, I realize things are forever changing: fashion, laws, global warming, politics, and even religious views. As the world continues to spin, what remains constant and factual is the control you have over yourself, the decisions you make, and your conscious mind. You can educate yourself, lose or gain weight, add value through finances, kids, and family, but what remains the same is your soul.

Protecting my energy, and consciously setting a will to stay positive, while believing in myself, has balanced my life in this chaotic world. I've seen a lot of artists, actors, and people fall to the poison of this world, but I have made a conscious decision to listen to the inner voice inside me. My intuitions are real, and it is the inner ability or insight to distinguish things without reason that keeps me going.

Your body will speak as long as you're lined up to hear.

I've said it in previous chapters, and it still remains the same; all doors that open are not meant to be entered. I advise that every opportunity is not meant to be acted upon. Trust your inner-self.

It may appear that everyone around you is surpassing you, but it's okay. Strategic, calculated moves are the key. You can alleviate many pitfalls and avoid spending money frivolously by listening to that quiet, still voice inside of you that nudges you when things, people, or situations are not right.

Setting goals and smashing them is the name of the game. Business plans, financial advisors, and classes are all things that prepare our life to succeed. The goal is to win.

The complexity begins when God starts to expand your territory. When I traverse unfamiliar territory, it is my faith and self-love that propels me to continue to put one foot in front of the other, while taking on projects and opportunities that were not in my plan.

Writing a book was something I had not envisioned, and it wasn't incorporated into my vision boards. My writing project was a sidebar and an opportunity that was presented through the network of people I have incorporated in my life.

Having an opportunity to reflect on my life and inspire others to live their best life is such a rewarding feeling.

When your vision consists of educating, empowering people, and helping birth millionaire mindsets, you have now entered into a BOSS life. Let's make this money and share the game so we all can be on the winning team. This is success to me.

All of my life, I had a passion for people, and I wasn't a loner. I made friends everywhere. Now, I am on a platform that I created; and the blueprint for the path that I plan to travel is mindblowing. Everyone and everything has a season and an expiration date. Since I have entered my new season, I've decided to bring some people along with me.

As for my millennials, I want you to give yourselves a break and relax. This topic typically does not apply to you. I need my twenty-year-veterans and my folks that took the same route as I did, going in full blast with a direction that you ultimately made a complete turn.

Fear, my friends, is what we all know. It is false evidence appearing real. Fear is a topic that we all can relate to. It causes us to delay and stop life and its hidden jewels. Fear is the opposite of faith, and you can't operate in fear and faith at the same time—something will cancel the other. Fear has caused many people to become stagnant in life. I don't want any of my readers to allow fear to control their destiny any longer.

We have to take hold of this dreadful disease and push through.

Take a deep breath and admit and recognize that this has been the hold-up. Educate yourself on whatever topic and situation that seems to have you paralyzed.

Sometimes, we are afraid of the unknown because of our lack of knowledge. Find your peace, visualize it, and set your mind on a positive track. Seek out help like support groups and get in the mix of that topic. Set a plan and take small steps forward, not a huge step, which could set you back.

I took steps with my friends walking in fear. I was so scared on some of those occasions, but I kept my feet moving. I chose to govern my life through faith, and with fear staring me in my eyes, I set myself up to win. Fear does not live here any longer. From this day forth, just like left and right is a part of our daily lives, so is fear or faith.

Let's Do it!

Will Smith and Tracey Moss on the set of Bad Boy3

CHAPTER 9

What's Next

Writing this book has released a desire in me to teach and inspire any that have a desire to dream. The completion of this book and me having a final copy in my hand is tangible evidence that all things are possible. God has truly blessed me, and I feel it is my responsibility to share my story to help you write and share your story.

You will see more of me through classes, seminars, and a host of media outlets. I am preparing myself for the next phase of public speaking. Yes, I said preparing. It was not on my vision list because I have always considered myself a hairstylist first. Like I mentioned earlier, my friends, we are taking strides together. I am no different from you.

Align yourself for success, open your mind to hear. Journaling your process is vital. There are many times in life that we lose sight, change directions, or sometimes just have a change of heart. Journaling helps with remembering, and many times, we get those nuggets down-loaded in us that we tend to forget.

My experiences on the set of TV and film productions have taught me some valuable life lessons. Everything is a learning experience; never take anything for granted. If you are in a particular season in your life, recognize what you need to receive from that moment.

While traveling life's journey, I had no idea everything I had accomplished and failed at would be the driving force for my success in TV and Film. Studying business administration was a prevision for film productions, and human resources were the introduction for people and understanding operations for productions and my brand. Working in the salon gave me a diverse foundation for styling hair, regardless of ethnicity. Working with production companies, music videos, and platform artistry has trained me to be creative, a quick thinker, and it has given me the ability to polish a look with confidence.

I am thankful to God for ordering my steps, for giving me the wisdom to connect the dots.

Life hasn't always been great. I've had trying times and closed doors. I've been let down and disappointed. TV and Film were not easy to embark on, and it's not all glitz and glamour. I'm thankful and will forever be grateful for this season in my life. Living life with regrets will cause one to be stagnant; it keeps you in a wishful state of mind. Yes, the statement, "If I knew then what I know now, I would have done a lot of things differently," is a very true statement, but life is too short to dwell on past mistakes.

If there were something that affected me to make or delay a decision, it would have been fear. Fear is something I had to be honest about and confront it head-on. Fear can cause your mind to play tricks on you. It will make you delusional. Life and opportunities will pass by, and you will remain in that bubble of fear.

I once heard a dynamic speaker that helped build my confidence, and it broke the spirit of fear in my life.

A man in regular, civilian clothes can go in the middle of a freeway and hold his arm up to stop traffic. He will succeed in stopping traffic for a short moment. Eventually, he will hear honks, see the middle finger, and more than likely hear, "Get out of the road, you moron!" Now, if the same man went to the same spot and held his hands out to stop traffic in a police uniform, with a badge, it would be perceived that he was assigned to do so, and is operating in his authority. He is accomplishing assignments with the confidence of his badge and the force behind him.

Once I got the revelation that God will never leave or forsake me, that my steps are ordered, that the joy of the Lord is my strength, I was able to walk in His authority. I no longer depend on Tracey Moss' strength and power alone. Life will honk at me and go around me, so I walk and trust the Lord.

Yes, life is complex, but examine whose authority you've been living in. Are you walking in your own power with million-dollar ideas? Are you bungee jumping in life with the hope that the rope won't break?

Take a minute and exhale, breathe, and give thanks for your journey. Be thankful for the good and the bad. Get under the authority of God; incorporate Him in your plan; wear the badge; declare your heart's desire for your life.